CHOICE

My Confirmation Journal

PAULIST PRESS
New York · Mahwah

I would like to thank Paulist Press for permission to reprint material from two of my earlier works, *Fastened on God* and *Prayers for a New Generation,* published by Paulist Press.

Scripture text in this book is from the *Good News Bible,* the Bible in Today's English Version. Copyright © American Bible Society 1966, 1971, 1976. Used by permission.

Library of Congress
Catalog Card Number: 86-60340

ISBN: 0-8091-9572-0

Published by Paulist Press
997 Macarthur Boulevard
Mahwah, New Jersey 07430

Printed and bound in the
United States of America

NAME _____

CONFIRMATION NAME _____

SPONSOR'S NAME _____

PARISH COMMUNITY _____

DATE OF CONFIRMATION _____

CELEBRATING BISHOP _____
(or representative)

About CHOICE

You are about to begin a process of deeper initiation into your Christian faith. You have already, of course, received God's life and Spirit because you are baptized. You also have received the nourishment of his body and blood in the Eucharist. Now you are about to receive the sacrament of Confirmation. If you were baptized as an infant you had little to say about that sacrament. But now, as our title indicates, you have the *choice* before you whether or not you wish to make a commitment as an emerging young adult, a commitment to the way of life as a Christian. God's action within your heart and soul will occur anyway when you receive Confirmation regardless of your level of commitment to the Christian life because God's Spirit is a total gift; but the more we are disposed to the reception of any sacrament, then the more filled up we are with the life of God.

While we feel that this choice properly belongs to you and that you should never be *forced* to receive a sacrament, we at the same time believe that only an *enlightened* and *informed* choice makes sense. That is why we support your parents and parish staff if they insist you participate in a Confirmation preparation process because that is the only way you'll be able to make an intelligent decision. That is why we have also designed this process over six months to give you time to think about what you are able to do. If after your retreat weekend you feel that you are not ready to receive this sacrament or make a commitment to the Church, then we have suggestions for you to deal with your choice at that time. But up until then we ask you to try to keep an open mind and to get as much as you can out of the sessions.

We call CHOICE a *process,* not a program. Why? Because it is not like a course from which you can graduate if you complete it successfully. To prepare for Confirmation is a process of reflection, review, soul-searching and sharing in order to ready your heart for the strengthening grace of the Holy Spirit. Confirmation is no graduation. In fact it's quite the opposite. It marks the beginning of living your Catholic faith in a more mature and adult way. It involves a commitment to following Jesus' way of life, to participating in the sacraments, to service to your brothers and sisters, and to ongoing religious education. Confirmation is also a gift of God's Spirit.

A sketch of the CHOICE process is as follows. Most of your preparation will be done in a small group which will become a Christian community, a miniature of the Church itself.

Sessions 1–6
A review of the kind of life Jesus calls us to live by looking at the Gospel

Sessions 8–11
A review of the basic doctrines of the Church

Sessions 14–19
Looking at your faith more deeply as a young person

There will also be liturgical services, a Parent–Youth Retreat, a Sponsor–Candidate Retreat, a Community Service project and a weekend retreat.

About Choosing a Sponsor

In the past, a Confirmation sponsor has been chosen to honor a family member or special adult who lived a good Catholic life. This is *not* the understanding of the sponsor's role today according to the revised rites of initiation in the Catholic Church. Your sponsor should be:

1. A Roman Catholic adult who practices his/her faith and is in good standing with the Church (ideally a member of your own parish community although this is not essential).

2. A "friend of your journey" toward Confirmation—someone you feel you can talk with on a personal level.

3. A person who you feel has something to offer you in terms of spiritual guidance, that is, one who lives a Christian lifestyle which you admire and would like to imitate in some degree.

A note about parents: Parents may not be sponsors of their own children at Confirmation according to new Church rules. This will help those teenagers who find it difficult to talk to their folks. It is quite normal during the teenage years to turn to a different adult other than one's parents for guidance or advice. Parents should understand that this is normal and healthy. But try to be sensitive to parents' feelings as we reshape the role of sponsor. Explain to your parents that in this process you don't "honor" someone by choosing him or her to be a sponsor. The sponsor is an adult from whom you feel you can receive some spiritual guidance and who is willing to make a commitment to you and to the process as well.

About Choosing a Confirmation Name

In the Bible, conversion to following God is often symbolized by a change in name: Abram becomes Abraham, Simon becomes Peter, Saul becomes Paul. At Baptism we receive a name to symbolize our new life in Christ. It probably makes the most sense to keep your own baptismal name at Confirmation after having done a little more research on the saint for whom your parents named you. If you wish, however, you may take a new symbolic name for Confirmation.

A bad reason to choose a new name:

Because you don't like your own name or because you like the sound of another name or because you want to honor a family member.

A good reason to choose a new name:

Because you have been impressed with the values of a saint about whom you have studied and read, and you wish to imitate that person in your own life—and you symbolize this by taking his or her name.

About Your Journal

This book is your special keepsake. You will use it for the CHOICE process. You are to bring it to every session, liturgy and retreat experience.

About the exercises for the group sessions. There are many scales, inventories, spectrums, etc. to stimulate group discussion. For these there are usually no right or wrong answers. Your score is only to help you see yourself in relationship to an issue or to other people to stir up some thought or discussion. *Whatever you do, don't be depressed by any of these results.* It may be just your mood at the time you took it. See the results as encouragement and challenge to growth.

About the New Testament

You will need to bring a New Testament to the first six sessions (we suggest the "Good News" edition). Your leader may request you to bring it at other times also.

How to read the New Testament:

The term "New Testament" refers to the second part of the Bible, which begins with the birth of Jesus Christ. The first part of the New Testament is called the Gospel, which literally means the "good news" of humankind's salvation by Jesus. There are four versions of the Gospel, written by four writers (called "evangelists"). They are Matthew, Mark, Luke, and John. Therefore a quote from a Gospel begins with the author's name and is followed by the chapter number and then the verse or verses from the chapter. For example, the Gospel of Luke, chapter ten, verses one through five is written: Luke 10:1-5.

After the four versions of the Gospel comes the "Acts of the Apostles," the story of the early Christian community. It is abbreviated as "Acts." After that comes the "epistles" or various letters of the early apostles to both communities and individuals. The majority of them were written by St. Paul. These are identified by the person or the community to whom they were written—for example, Ephesians 2:12 or Titus 2:15. When more than one epistle is written to the same community it is preceded by a number—for example, 2 Thessalonians 3:17. The epistles *not* written by St. Paul are identified by the authors: James, Peter, John and Jude. The final section of the New Testament is the Book of Revelation which is very symbolic and written about the end of time. It is very difficult to understand without proper guidance.

INITIAL QUESTIONNAIRE

(Fill in the following briefly before you discuss.)

1. What places have you lived? Have you always resided at the same address?

2. What is some hobby or interest that you have?

3. What is your *least* favorite subject in school?

4. Do you have any feelings about your previous religious education?

5. Do you have any goals for yourself in this Confirmation process? Is there something that you hope you can get out of it?

6. On a scale of one to ten what place would you say that your religious faith has in your life (that is, "one" being the least important aspect and "ten" being the most important aspect)?

Doctrinal Summary

BAPTISM

1. Baptism is a sacrament, a special encounter with Jesus Christ.

2. Baptism consists in the words: "I baptize you _____(name)_____ in the name of the Father, the Son and the Holy Spirit"—as well as immersion in or the pouring of water. The ordinary minister is a deacon or priest but in an emergency any baptized Christian may baptize another.

3. Baptism is the first step in Christian initiation into God's family, the Church community, and expresses our belief in Jesus as our Lord.

4. The result of Baptism is that we are free to go to heaven when we die to be with God forever and also that we are members of the Christian community.

EXERCISE #1
COMMUNITY

Complete the following briefly and then share your answers with your group:

1. What for you is the hardest part of "breaking into" a new group?

2. Are there cliques or divisions in your school? Do you see yourself in a certain group?

3. What do you feel is necessary to break down cliques to form a community?

4. Do you feel your parish is a community? Do you feel a part of it?

EXERCISE #2
POWER WITHIN

Glue your baby picture to this space as a symbol of the person you were at the time of your Baptism.

Answer the following questions briefly and then share them with your group.

1. Do you ever think about the fact that you are baptized or do you take it for granted?

2. You have changed physically and emotionally since this picture was taken. How have you changed "spiritually" since you were younger? Do you think of God differently now?

3. Do you ever think of God living within you?

4. Is there a time you feel you could share with your group when God was really "with you"?

EXERCISE #1
HOW FAR WILL YOU GO?

Read the list of items below. Ask yourself this question for each item: "Whom would you lend it to?" Then put a check mark under the correct heading according to your answer. You may check more than one answer for each.

	Best friend	Brother or sister	Classmate	Someone you dislike	No one
Favorite CD	_____	_____	_____	_____	_____
New clothes	_____	_____	_____	_____	_____
Your paycheck	_____	_____	_____	_____	_____
Skis	_____	_____	_____	_____	_____
New tennis racket	_____	_____	_____	_____	_____
Your car	_____	_____	_____	_____	_____

EXERCISE #2
EXAMINE YOUR HEART

This exercise requires a few moments of silence. There is no need to write the answers unless you care to. Only share with your group as much as you feel comfortable sharing. The important thing is to be honest with yourself.

1. Who is the person (if any) toward whom you feel some degree of revenge?

2. Apart from what happened between you, what emotion did you experience as a result of that unpleasant interaction? Have you acknowledged this emotion to yourself before?

3. Which member of your family do you find it most difficult to love and respect?

4. What concrete, practical resolution can you make right now to become a more loving human being?

THE FINAL JUDGMENT

We can understand the images Jesus presents here in a physical way or in a psychological way. The physical is obvious and easy to grasp and certainly demands our attention. For example, each of us should actively be concerned about physical hunger in the world. But people can have other hungers too: for attention, for understanding, for affection, for friendship, etc. Take the images below and try to explore as a group in discussion a broader sense to each of these terms:

> thirst
> being a stranger
> nakedness
> sickness
> imprisonment

Do you see your Christian calling as a responsibility to meet all these physical and spiritual needs of other people?

Does this description by Jesus of the "last judgment" conform to your own ideas of how God will judge you? If it differs, how does it differ? Share this with your group.

SELF-IN-COMMUNITY SYMBOL

MATERIALS: crayons or magic markers. In this block draw a symbol of your personal "community"—your social network of family, friends and acquaintances. Use symbolic designs and colors. In some way let one of the symbols represent you in relationship to your "people-world." Explain your drawing to the group.

EXERCISE #1
HOW MUCH TRUST DO YOU HAVE?
(IN PEOPLE)

Read each question. Circle your answer.	Yes	No	Maybe
1. Would you discuss a personal problem with your best friend?	Y	N	M
2. Would you share a secret with a brother or sister?	Y	N	M
3. Would you lend your favorite CD to any person who asked?	Y	N	M
4. Would you forgive someone who apologized for starting a rumor about you?	Y	N	M
5. Would you accept a ride with a stranger?	Y	N	M
6. Would you tell your parents you smoked at a party (when they have forbidden this)?	Y	N	M
7. Would you talk to your parents about a sex problem or question?	Y	N	M
8. Would you talk to a teacher about something bothering you?	Y	N	M
9. Would you tell your best friend he or she had bad breath?	Y	N	M
10. Would you fall in love easily?	Y	N	M
11. Would you doubt your friendship if you didn't hear from your best friend in two days?	Y	N	M
12. Would you be afraid to give your best friend constructive criticism?	Y	N	M
13. Would you doubt your doctor's diagnosis if he told you that you had a serious disease?	Y	N	M
14. Would you believe a compliment if you received one?	Y	N	M
15. Would you tell someone about something you are very ashamed of?	Y	N	M

EXERCISE #2
HOW MUCH TRUST DO YOU HAVE?
(IN GOD)

Read each question. Circle your answer.	Yes	No	Maybe
1. Would you talk over a personal problem with God?	Y	N	M
2. Would you feel God's love even after you did something wrong?	Y	N	M
3. Would you believe that God cares about your life?	Y	N	M
4. Would you feel that God cares about you when you're feeling down and depressed?	Y	N	M
5. Would you feel forgiven of your sins if you received the sacrament of Reconciliation?	Y	N	M
6. Would you have gotten all the way to Jesus if you had been in Peter's place?	Y	N	M
7. Would you turn to the Bible for some comforting words in a stressful time?	Y	N	M
8. Would you turn to Jesus in prayer for a family member or friend who was sick or in trouble?	Y	N	M
9. Would you talk to a priest or some other adult in a ministerial role about a problem you were having?	Y	N	M
10. Would you turn to God for guidance in making a difficult decision?	Y	N	M

Adding up your responses and sharing your totals with your group might help you to see yourself more objectively as a trusting or mistrustful person. There are probably parallels in your trust in people and your trust in God. Trust is something we learn very early in life from our parents (who also represent God to us). If you feel you need to be more trusting don't expect to change overnight. Ask Jesus in prayer to help you trust in him more. Take a risk in sharing something you feel you need to speak about with a friend (or even in this group). It's the taking of risks in life and in prayer that gradually builds up our trust.

"MY BARN"

For this man it was a question of storing grain. Today for many of us it would be having a savings account and hoarding money. But as teenagers there are often other items, material goods, of which we are very possessive. There are non-material realities (such as power, friends, fame) which we also tend to accumulate. What for you, besides money, would be the "grain" which you store in *your* "barn"? Discuss this with your group.

If you have time also read the story of Lazarus in Luke 16:19–31.

LIST 4 MATERIAL GOODS OF WHICH YOU ARE POSSESSIVE

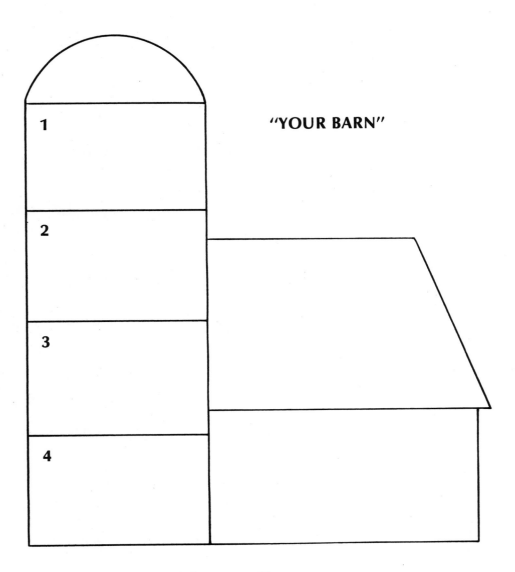

"YOUR BARN"

TRUST MEDITATION

Close your eyes and listen to the gospel read at the beginning of tonight's session read again. Try to imagine the event through the eyes of Peter . . . pretend to yourself that *you* are the one invited to step out in faith. How would you have felt? . . . What would you have done? Share the answers to these questions below with your group.

1. How would you feel and react if you were out in a boat with your friends and all of a sudden a storm rose up and the wind and waves started rocking your small vessel?

2. If, caught in this storm, you saw Jesus standing on the water in the distance . . . how would you react?

3. If Jesus invited you to come out to him by walking on the water, what would you do?

4. If you did in fact start walking toward Jesus and the wind started to blow fiercely, would that affect you?

5. Has there ever been a real situation in your life where the "storm" of human events caused you to doubt God's care for you?

WORRY SPECTRUM

Place yourself on the continuum below by writing your first name on the line where you feel you *usually* fall relative to anxiety. Those in the group closer to the "cool" "calm" end should share how they handle life's concerns with the rest.

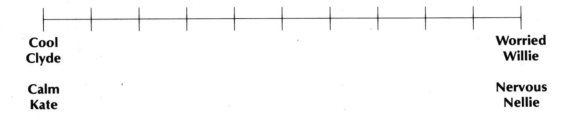

Cool   **Worried**
Clyde   **Willie**

Calm   **Nervous**
Kate   **Nellie**

For additional group discussion:

1. Does worry ever change anything?

2. Is today's generation too concerned about their material welfare?

3. Is financial success at the top of *your* list of goods?

4. Do you really believe that the Lord cares about you in all the details of your life?

5. Do you perceive any value to suffering in your life?

"SELF-EULOGY"

Write below a eulogy (a sermon) about yourself that you would like to hear delivered by someone about you at your own funeral. Include in it all the things you *hope* to attain during your lifetime. After you have completed it trade it with one other member of your group and read each other's eulogies privately. Do this exercise in a serious way.

After the eulogies have been written and exchanged, share your responses to these sentences with the members of your group:

Sentence Completion

If I were to die soon, it would be important to me that people

thought I _____

After I die, I want people to remember my _____

_____

When I die, I hope people _____

_____

SENTENCE COMPLETERS

In your group go around in a circle, each member completing the next sentence. Do not react during this process. After each statement has been completed go back and ask anyone you wish to explain his/her sentence. You will notice how individually we react to various forms of suffering.

If I were bedridden in a body cast for six months, I'd

If I were handicapped and had to be in a wheelchair all the time I'd

If my face became badly and permanently scarred in a car accident I'd

If my brother or sister took an overdose I'd

If one of my parents committed suicide I'd

If my family was very poor and we had only one meal a day I'd

If I became a widow or widower at age 28 and had 2 small children I'd

If I lost my leg in a car accident I'd

If I flunked all my subjects in school and had to repeat the year I'd

If I were attacked and beaten up badly I'd

If I were a parent and had a retarded child I'd

If a gang attacked and killed one of my parents I'd

If I broke my neck in a swimming accident and became paralyzed I'd

If I were a new parent and my first baby died I'd

If my best friend rejected and dropped me I'd

If I were blind I'd

If I found out I had cancer and had six months to live I'd

If I injured my leg in a football accident and had to wear a brace for the rest of my life I'd

If I lost a pet that was important to me I'd

MY PERSONAL PRAYER DESCRIPTIONS

Complete and share your answers with your group:

1. For me, prayer is like the noun _____ .

2. For me, prayer is like the verb _____ .

3. For me, prayer is like the adjective _____ .

4. When I pray my mental picture is of: _____

   _____ .

5. My favorite spot to pray is: _____ .

6. My best time of day to pray is: _____ .

7. My favorite type of prayer is: _____

   _____ .

8. What percentage (1%–100%) of your prayer is spent listening to the Lord? _____ .

9. The person who taught me to pray was _____ .

10. The thing I'd most like to learn about prayer is: _____

    _____

    _____ .

"BEATITUDINAL PROFILE"

Put a dot on the spot on the spectrum where you feel you *usually* fall. Then draw a line connecting the dots to get your profile. Discuss yourself in relationship to each beatitude with your group.

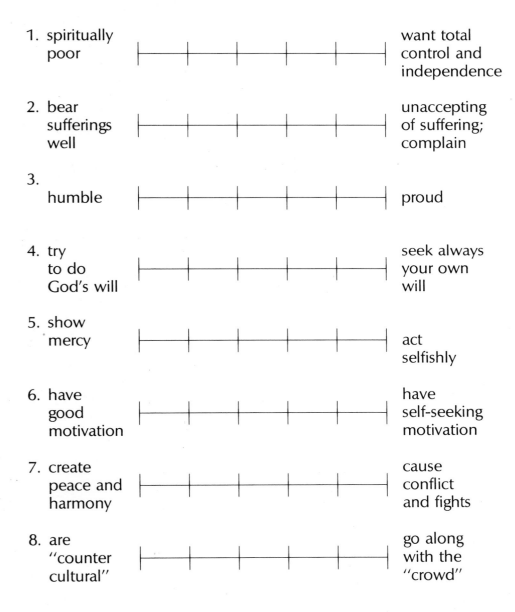

1. spiritually poor ————————————— want total control and independence

2. bear sufferings well ————————————— unaccepting of suffering; complain

3. humble ————————————— proud

4. try to do God's will ————————————— seek always your own will

5. show mercy ————————————— act selfishly

6. have good motivation ————————————— have self-seeking motivation

7. create peace and harmony ————————————— cause conflict and fights

8. are "counter cultural" ————————————— go along with the "crowd"

LETTER TO JESUS

In the space below write a personal letter to Jesus as you would write to any friend. For the closing prayer of this session, share *one sentence* of your choice from this letter with your group.

Dear Jesus,

Signed:

Rite of Choice

Presentation of Candidates: (by D.R.E. or youth minister, president of the parish council or you, the group leader) Stand facing pastor in sanctuary.

"Father _____(pastor's name)_____ , I present to you the members of our parish community preparing for the sacrament of Confirmation. Already having been baptized into Christ they choose today to follow Jesus more closely by entering into a catechetical preparation for this sacrament. To help them in this process they turn to you our leader and the parish community of _(name of parish)_ for support, encouragement and guidance."

Pastor: "Members of this parish community, you have heard the request for our guidance and support. Are you willing to help these young people by your witness of Christian living and by your prayers?"

Congregation: "We are."

Pastor: "Parents and sponsors present here today, are you willing to give that special encouragement these candidates will need from you in their continuing Christian journey?"

Congregation: "We are."

(Confirmation candidates stand.)

Pastor: "Confirmation candidates, do you make a special choice today to embark in a process of intensive catechetical preparation for the sacrament of Confirmation?"

Candidates: "We do."

Pastor: "Do you freely choose to try to follow the Gospel teachings which you have been reviewing?"

Candidates: "We do."

Pastor: "Do you promise to study, to pray, to serve, and to build community in order to become a young adult witness to Jesus Christ?"

Candidates: "We do."

Pastor: "Take and receive this light from our parish paschal candle (he takes his taper to the paschal candle and extends it to the first candidate who lights the next candidate's, etc., in a "chain-like" fashion) as a symbol of your choice to become a witness to Jesus Christ, the light that has come into this world to dispel the darkness of sin and death. May you burn with love for him and all your brothers and sisters in this world."

(After the last taper has been lit the pastor continues)

"We, the parish of _____(name of parish)_____ , pledge to support you in your decision and look forward to the day of your Confirmation when you share with us more fully in Christian adulthood." (Congregation applauds)

Synopsis of Hebrew Scriptures (Old Testament)

"Hebrew salvation history" began around 1850 B.C. when God brought Abraham, leader of the "Habiru" tribe, into a realization that there is but one God (monotheism). Prior to this people believed in many gods. We think Abraham's tribe may have worshiped the moon. Abraham was told to take his people away from the city of Ur (present day Iraq), away from pagan influence, to a promised land that God (called "Yahweh") would show him. Abraham had great faith and trusted God to lead him and his people. We call this bond of trust between Abraham and God the "covenant"—i.e., if people are faithful to God, God will care for them. The Hebrew tribe is later led by Abraham's son Isaac and Isaac's son Jacob. Jacob's son is the famous Joseph who gets carried into slavery in Egypt. During a widespread famine the entire Hebrew tribe is forced to go into Egypt for food where they eventually become the slaves of Pharaoh. All these events from Abraham to Joseph are contained in the first book of the Bible called Genesis. The Jews were in Egypt from about 1700 to 1220 B.C.

In the Book of Exodus we read the famous story of Moses, a Hebrew raised as an Egyptian who was inspired by God to lead his people out of slavery into freedom (called the exodus). Pharaoh, frightened by the famous ten plagues, finally lets the Hebrews go. Moses leads them into the desert where God gives them food and water. In the desert the covenant gets more detailed in the Ten Commandments which Moses is inspired to write down on Mount Sinai.

Upon the death of Moses the Hebrews finally reach the promised land (Canaan—present day Israel) and are led across the Jordan River by their new leader, Joshua. The tribe is led by military leaders called judges until close to 1000 B.C. when the tribe has grown to a nation and the need for a king is felt by the people. Saul is the first king and David is the second. David establishes a capital in Jerusalem and under its strong leadership the nation enjoys a brief "golden period." Solomon succeeds David and builds the great temple. After Solomon the nation weakens and becomes victimized by various military conquests. In 932 B.C. the nation divides into two kingdoms, Israel and Judah. Israel in the north crumbles in 721 B.C. and Judah falls in 586 B.C. with the Babylonian conquest. During this span of four hundred years we have the rise of the great religious prophets.

Below are the Ten Commandments for your memorization:

THE TEN COMMANDMENTS

1. I am the Lord your God. I brought you out of the land of Egypt. You shall honor no other God but me.

2. You shall not misuse the name of the Lord your God.

3. Remember to keep holy the sabbath day.

4. Honor your father and your mother.

5. You shall not kill.

6. You shall not commit adultery.

7. You shall not steal.

8. You shall not bear false witness against your neighbor.

9. You shall not covet your neighbor's wife.

10. You shall not covet your neighbor's goods.

A SOUL-SEARCH:
ME AND THE TEN COMMANDMENTS

Complete the following:

1. A "false god" I have is:

2. A word I have the bad habit of saying is:

3. A poor excuse I've used to miss Mass on Sunday:

4. A way I don't honor my parents:

5. A way I sometimes "kill" people:

6. A way I am unfaithful to a friend:

7. A way I steal:

8. A way I lie:

9/10. Some jealousy I have:

Admittedly these are very personal questions. For that reason share only those you feel comfortable about sharing with your group.

MY TEN COMMANDMENTS

If you were God what are ten rules that you would devise for all people to follow for all time? Upon completion share these in your group.

1.

2.

3.

4.

5.

6.

7.

8.

9.

10.

THE SEVEN SACRAMENTS

SACRAMENT	SYMBOL	EFFECT
1. Baptism	Pouring or immersion in water; words of Baptism	Receive grace; enter Christian community
2. Confirmation	Laying on of hands and anointing with oil	The completion of Baptism
3. Holy Eucharist	Partaking of bread and wine at liturgy	Receive Jesus Christ as our spiritual food
4. Reconciliation	Words of absolution by the priest; sign of the cross	Sins forgiven
5. Anointing of the Sick	Anointing sick person on the forehead and arms	Healing and consoling power of Jesus received
6. Holy Orders (Ordination)	Laying on of hands by bishop	Persons chosen to be special ministers to the Christian community
7. Matrimony	The exchange of the vows of marriage by a husband and wife	A lasting commitment between two people which is a symbol of Christ's union with the Church

To discuss with your leader during this session:

1. Which sacrament do you understand the least and requires more explanation?

2. Which sacrament means the most to you in your life right now?

3. What does it mean to say that we can be "sacraments" for each other?

AWARENESS

Sacraments are invisible realities which call upon our awareness to the movement of God's Spirit. How aware are you of the reality around you? Most of us are so caught up in our everyday preoccupations that we miss out on a large portion of reality. Test your awareness by doing the following exercise:

1. Close your eyes. (Ask someone to read #2–#10 to you.)

2. Get in a comfortable position. (Lie on the floor if there is room and if it is carpeted.)

3. Take a few deep breaths. (pause)

4. Be aware of any sounds around you. (pause)

5. Be aware of your own breathing. (pause)

6. Be aware of any feeling going on within you. (pause)

7. If any distracting thoughts come into your imagination, gently let them go. (pause)

8. Remember Jesus' words that "the kingdom of God is within you." (pause)

9. Concentrate on the Spirit of God actually living within your own body. (extra-long pause)

10. Say a short prayer within yourself that you will grow in the awareness of God's life within you.

The Apostles' Creed

I believe in God, the Father almighty, Creator of heaven and earth;
and in Jesus Christ, his only Son, our Lord;
who was conceived by the Holy Spirit,
born of the Virgin Mary,
suffered under Pontius Pilate,
was crucified, died, and was buried.
He descended into hell; the third day he arose again from the dead.
He ascended into heaven, sits at the right hand of God, the Father
      almighty;
from thence he shall come to judge the living and the dead.
I believe in the Holy Spirit,
the holy Catholic Church,
the communion of saints,
the forgiveness of sins,
the resurrection of the body, and life everlasting, Amen.

This summary of our Catholic beliefs should be memorized if you do not know it already.

"MY CREED"

Write a short paragraph about your own values in life—what you cherish to be true in addition to the Apostles' Creed. For your closing prayer to this session share your "creed" with your group.

Catholic Identity: Important Definitions

Our identity as Roman Catholic Christians is unique. As discussed in the Creed we trace ourselves to Peter and the apostles. Our faith is based upon God's revelation in *Scripture* as well as *tradition* which is the practice of the Church community down through the ages. Our identity is also manifested in our religious terminology and doctrinal definitions—these reflect our self-understanding. Let's begin with some terms we just discussed in the Creed:

1. *Trinity*—The mystery of three persons in one God: Father, Son and Holy Spirit

2. *Incarnation*—God becoming man in Jesus Christ

3. *Redemption*—Jesus' saving act for humanity through his death on the cross

4. *Resurrection*—Jesus being raised from the dead three days after his death on the cross

5. *Ascension*—Jesus' return to heaven forty days after his resurrection

6. *Immaculate Conception*—The belief that the Virgin Mary was conceived in her mother's womb without original sin

7. *Assumption*—The belief that the Virgin Mary was immediately assumed into heaven after her death

8. *Hierarchy*—The name given to leadership in the Church: the Pope, the supreme head of the Church, successor to St. Peter, and the bishops who lead the various dioceses throughout the world

9. *Liturgy*—the official worship of God by the Church through the Mass, sacraments and other rites of the Church as contained in its official books

10. *Rosary*—a special series of prayers honoring the Virgin Mary while meditating on the mysteries in her life and in Jesus' life

Other important Roman Catholic definitions:

Precepts of the Church

1. Participate in the Sunday Eucharist and refrain from unnecessary work on the sabbath.

2. Receive Holy Communion during Eastertime.

3. Confess serious sins at least once a year.

4. Observe the marriage laws of the Church.

5. Help support the Church.

6. Do penance, abstaining from meat and fasting from food on the appointed days.

7. Join the missionary spirit and apostolate of the church.

The Corporal Works of Mercy

1. Feed the hungry.
2. Give drink to the thirsty.
3. Clothe the naked.
4. Shelter the homeless.
5. Visit the sick.
6. Visit the imprisoned.
7. Bury the dead.

The Spiritual Works of Mercy

1. Convert the sinner.
2. Instruct the ignorant.
3. Counsel the doubtful.
4. Comfort the sorrowful.
5. Bear wrongs patiently.
6. Forgive injuries.
7. Pray for the living and the dead.

The Capital Sins

1. Pride
2. Covetousness
3. Lust
4. Anger
5. Gluttony
6. Envy
7. Sloth

DOUBT LIST

Write down three things—doctrines, rules or teachings of the Catholic faith—which you find either confusing, erroneous or hard to accept.

1.

2.

3.

Share these with your group. Maybe others can clarify something you don't understand. If confusion persists after this session, discuss your question with someone who has a background in theology, such as your parish priest or director of religious education. It's important to do this sort of clarifying while preparing for confirmation.

Seasons of the Church Year

- *The Church Year.* Throughout each year, Christians celebrate the mystery of Jesus' life, death and resurrection, beginning with Advent. We also commemorate saints and some important events in Mary's life during the Church year.

- *Sunday.* Each Sunday we celebrate the paschal mystery of Jesus' death and resurrection. We follow a tradition which began with the apostles who celebrated the first day of the week, the "Lord's Day," because it was the day of Jesus' resurrection.

- *Advent.* The season of Advent lasts about four weeks and takes place prior to Christmas. It is a season of spiritual expectation which emphasizes our need to prepare for the coming of the Lord at Christmas as well as our hope that he will come again.

- *Christmas Season.* Christmas celebrates the birth of our Lord. The Christmas season lasts until Epiphany. Epiphany commemorates Jesus' first manifestation to the Gentile world, when he was visited by the magi.

- *Lent.* The Season of Lent is a six week period during which we prepare for the celebration of Easter. It is a time of penance and renewal. During Lent we try to reform our lives and live in a way that is more faithful to the gospel.

- *The Easter Triduum.* The three most important celebrations of the liturgical year: the Mass of the Lord's Supper on Holy Thursday, the celebration of the Passion on Good Friday, and the Easter Vigil during the night of Holy Saturday. Together these liturgies celebrate the heart of our faith, the death and resurrection of Christ.

- *The Easter Season.* The celebration of Easter lasts for fifty days—from Easter to Pentecost. This is an extended time of celebration of the resurrection and the beginning of the Church. It includes the feasts of Jesus' Ascension into heaven and Pentecost which marks the descent of the Holy Spirit on the apostles.

- *Ordinary Time.* These are the Sundays and weekdays apart from the special seasons of the year. Each Sunday is a celebration of the resurrection and the gospels of these Sundays look at different moments in Jesus' life and ministry.

EXERCISE #1
"MY PATIENCE BAROMETER"

Advent is a time of waiting when we focus upon patient expectation.
Rate yourself on a scale from 1 to 10 relative to the statements below:

"1" = very patient   "10" = very impatient

(The way you *usually* are in these various situations.)

1. To wait for a red light I am   _____

2. When I am waiting for supper I am   _____

3. When I am with small children I am   _____

4. When I am with old people I am   _____

5. When I am waiting for a test grade I am   _____

6. When I am dressing/grooming I am   _____

7. When I have a lot of work to do I am   _____

8. When I play sports I am   _____

9. When I am alone in the house I am   _____

10. When I am with my friends I am   _____

11. When I am attending Sunday Mass I am   _____

12. When I talk with my parents I am   _____

13. When undertaking a new task I am   _____

14. When I eat food I am   _____

15. When I think about my future I am   _____

TOTAL: _____

Add up your score. Share/discuss your total with your group.

EXERCISE #2

In Lent we practice penance or "asceticism." By doing so we learn self-control and prepare our hearts for deeper prayer. Try to practice one form of self-control or sacrifice this week. Write your resolution in the space below to help you to concretize it. Be sure to be specific.

This week I will try . . .

Signed _____
(your name)

LENT

Answer the questions below and then share your answers with your group.

1. If the church did not celebrate Lent do you think we would ever think about Jesus Christ dying for us?

2. Do you think that it is important that we reflect on his death? Why or why not?

3. Does everyone who truly gives of himself or herself to another "die" in some way through the giving? Explain.

4. What are some examples of sacrifice that parents make?

   That people your age make?

5. How do you feel when you have sacrificed something for another person?

SERVICE PROJECT REFLECTION SHEET

Date of Service _____ Place _____

Write your responses briefly and share them with your group.

1. Before the project how did you feel about going?

2. How did you feel right after the project?

3. Do you see the project connected in any way to your Confirmation process? How?

4. Did the project have any negative parts to it for you?

5. Is there any practical resolution you can make as a result of this project?

SELF-IMAGE INVENTORY

Next to each statement below put:
    4—if the statement is completely true;
    3—if it's usually true;
    2—if it's partly true;
    1—if it's hardly ever true;
    0—if it's untrue.

1. _____ I like my home.
2. _____ I deserve the best.
3. _____ My life is interesting.
4. _____ I wouldn't trade places with anybody.
5. _____ I have my whole life before me to do as I wish.
6. _____ I feel comfortable with people.
7. _____ I'm attractive.
8. _____ I'm not afraid to say what I think.
9. _____ People value what I say.
10. _____ I'm going to heaven.
11. _____ There isn't much I'd change about the way I look.
12. _____ People care for me.
13. _____ I wouldn't change too much about my life.
14. _____ God really loves me.
15. _____ I'm an upbeat person.
16. _____ I can laugh at myself when I goof up.
17. _____ I have energy and zest for life.
18. _____ I'm seldom depressed.
19. _____ I have the number of friends I want.
20. _____ People like to be my friends.
21. _____ The opposite sex could be attracted to me.
22. _____ I'm not really ashamed of anything.
23. _____ I enjoy my daily life.
24. _____ I basically like what I see in the mirror.
25. _____ I enjoy starting each new day.
26. _____ I'm usually in a pretty good mood.
27. _____ I'm enjoyable to be with.
28. _____ I have very few regrets.
29. _____ I'm a kind, caring type of person.
30. _____ I'm unique.
    _____ TOTAL

Now add up your column and follow this key:

95   If you've answered truthfully you have a very good self-image. Congratulations!

70–95   You really like yourself enough to make it in this life. You know you're not perfect but you believe in yourself.

48–70   You have a mixture of feelings but probably focus too much on your weak points. But you can change if you want to!

below 48   You're not too happy with yourself and probably have an inaccurate self-image. You should talk to a friend or a group of friends or a teacher or counselor to see how *they* perceive you. You're probably selling yourself short!

With as much courage as you can muster, share your scores with your group.

Doctrinal Connector: Love is the theological virtue that causes us to love God above all things and to love our neighbor for the sake of God *as we love ourselves.* "Self-love" sometimes means selfishness which pulls us away from God and neighbor. But a healthy self-image means we respect our goodness because we were created by God and because we are the object of his love.

WINDOWS TO MYSELF

Answer the questions in each windowpane and then share them with your group.

How my friends see me:	**How my parents see me:**
How my teachers see me:	**How I see myself:**

WHO IS YOUR GOD?

(Check whichever applies)

_____ A judge	_____ An energy
_____ A concerned father	_____ A lawgiver
_____ A close friend	_____ A "feeling" inside a person
_____ A very vague being	_____ Perfection
_____ A protector	_____ Jesus
_____ An historical figure	_____ A huge computer
_____ A friend	_____ A magical power
_____ A distant figure	_____ A giver of gifts
_____ A policeman	_____ Non-existent
_____ In people	_____ Someone to talk to

WHERE IS YOUR GOD?

(Check only the one which most of the time is the way you feel)

_____ Up in heaven	_____ In other people
_____ Invisibly near you	_____ In church
_____ In your heart	_____ Somewhere else
_____ In the tabernacle	_____ Wherever friends gather

1. Share your responses with your group. Have your views of God shifted in the last five years? If so, also explain how you used to see him as opposed to the way you see him now.

2. Has anyone in whom you have had faith ended up disappointing you? Has this affected your relationship with God?

3. Do you think of faith more as belief that God exists or *living* in a way that you know God is with you?

Doctrinal Connector: Like hope and love, faith is a "theological" virtue, the essentials of the spiritual life according to St. Paul (1 Thessalonians 1:3; 5:8; 1 Corinthians 13:13). It is a gift of God to the individual. The Church distinguishes it from but connects it to "morals" or behavior. Revealed truths are believed in faith and move us to the way God wants us to live. The Church also distinguishes between faith and reason. These are not at odds, but faith means we believe without perceptible proof. Lastly the Church connects faith with good works or action. "Faith without actions is dead" (James 2:26).

"MY SPIRITUAL JOURNEY"

In this space below thoughtfully write about your life with God since your childhood. When was it close? When did you drift away? How has your understanding of his relationship with you evolved? How is your "spiritual life" going at the present time? You will be invited, not required, to share this with your group.

Doctrinal Connector: "Grace" is the term used in theology to describe God's favor to human persons. The "state of grace" refers to the spiritual life into which those recipients of God's favor come. "Actual grace" refers to an internal strengthening we receive at a particular time when we need God's help. "Habitual grace" refers to the supernatural gift of God which places a person in a state of permanent friendship with him. This "friendship with God" is the spiritual life.

Some Ancient Prayers and Customs
A Catholic Should Know

Sign of the Cross

In the name of the Father,
and of the Son,
and of the Holy Spirit.
Amen.

The Lord's Prayer

Our Father, who art in heaven,
hallowed be thy name.
Thy kingdom come; thy will be done
on earth as it is in heaven.
Give us this day our daily bread,
and forgive us our trespasses
as we forgive those who trespass
against us.
Lead us not into temptation
but deliver us from evil.
Amen.
(optional ending)
For thine is the kingdom
and the power
and the glory forever.
Amen.

Doxology

Glory to the Father,
and to the Son,
and to the Holy Spirit.
As it was in the beginning,
is now, and ever shall be,
world without end.
Amen.

Hail Mary

Hail, Mary, full of grace,
the Lord is with thee.
Blessed art thou among women,
and blessed is the fruit
of thy womb, Jesus.
Holy Mary, Mother of God,
pray for us sinners, now,
and at the hour of death.
Amen.

The Rosary

(already discussed in Session 6)

Benediction

A paraliturgical Eucharistic service which began in the fourteenth century. The consecrated bread, the "Blessed Sacrament," is exposed from the tabernacle where it is preserved for public adoration. The use of incense and sacred songs are a part of the service.

Stations of the Cross

The name of the devotion practiced by Catholics commonly on Fridays and during Lent. The person moves around the church (every Catholic church has Stations) to fourteen crosses or images depicting the passion and death of Jesus and prays and meditates at each.

HOW DEEP IS YOUR FAITH?

In your New Testament read the parable of the sower in Matthew 13: 1–9. After that, read all four descriptions of "soil." Think about each and choose the description that fits you best. Then discuss your choice with your group.

I'M ROCKY SOIL.   I have little or no depth. At times I do get excited about doing good for somebody or about being a Christian, but my excitement usually doesn't last long. Sometimes the gospel can even turn me on, but I soon forget all about it.

I'M THORNY SOIL.   I believe in what Jesus teaches as long as it doesn't cramp my style. I want to live a good life, but pressure usually keeps me from doing it. I hate to be criticized and made fun of, and so often worry about what other people think. And then, I don't usually stick to my beliefs.

I'M THE PATH.   I never even hear the word of God, much less read it. Even if I do go to church I don't listen to the readings. They're boring. They're not important. They go in one ear and out the other.

I'M GOOD SOIL.   At least I try to be. I do listen to the readings at Mass, and I usually try to live a good life. Jesus' teachings mean a lot to me, and so I try to take them seriously. I do ask God's help sometimes when I'm finding it hard to be Christian—for instance, when it's hard to make a decision about right or wrong. I'm far from perfect, but I do try to be a Christian.

Models of the Church

MODEL	PURPOSE	MISSION
Community	To unite all members into the "body of Christ"	To seek deeper union with God and all other people
Herald	Emphasizes the Bible, God's word	To proclaim the "good news" to the world
Institution	To provide structure, order and guidance for Church members	To teach, to rule and make holy
Sacrament	Reminds the Church of what it is called to be	To be a meaningful sign of God's love to all people
Servant	To serve the needs of society, especially the poor, weak and suffering	To renew the earth with the viewpoint of Jesus Christ

Doctrinal Connector: The Catholic Church is the family of God on earth which a person is born into by baptism. Its purpose is to build up the kingdom of God on earth in a community of love. It is also called the "mystical body of Christ." A beautiful and significant description of the Church can be found in the Dogmatic Constitution on the Church from the documents of Vatican Council II.

Synopsis of Highlights of Church History

DATE		
About 29 A.D.	Pentecost	Birth of the Church; Acts of the Apostles in the New Testament recounts early Christian history
313	Edict of Milan	Religious persecution ends
317	Arianism (heresy) appears	Teaches Jesus was not divine/God
325	Council of Nicea—the Creed is written	Arianism is condemned
431	Council of Ephesus	Refutes heresy of Nestorianism which denied Mary to be Mother of God
800	Pope Leo III crowns Charlemagne as emperor	A fusion between Church and state
1049	Pope Leo IX elected	Church reform begins; frees Church from control of kings and feudal lords
1054	Schism ("separation") between Church of West (Rome) and East (Constantinople)	Disagreement over liturgical practices; this schism remains today— the Eastern churches are called "Orthodox"
1095	First Crusade	Christians attack Moslems to recapture the Holy Land
1521	Diet of Worms ("diet" means parliament of the German empire; "Worms" was a city in southern Germany)	Martin Luther leads a "protest," a "reformation" of abuses in church by breaking with Rome
1545	Council of Trent	Catholic Church reforms itself by ridding abuses
1870	First Vatican Council	Dogma of papal infallibility: that when the Pope speaks to the whole Church in Christ's name he is kept from error in matters of faith and morality
1962	Second Vatican Council	Many changes to bring the Church into the modern world
1978	Pope John Paul II	Election of new Pope by college of cardinals (the group of bishops chosen to especially assist the Pope)

I may be able to speak the languages of men and even of angels, but if I have no love, my speech is no more than a noisy gong or a clanging bell. I may have the gift of inspired preaching; I may have all knowledge and understand all secrets; I may have all the faith needed to move mountains—but if I have no love, I am nothing. I may give away everything I have, and even give up my body to be burned—but if I have no love, this does me no good.

Love is patient and kind; it is not jealous or conceited or proud; love is not ill-mannered or selfish or irritable; love does not keep a record of wrongs; love is not happy with evil, but is happy with the truth. Love never gives up, and its faith, hope, and patience never fail.

1 Corinthians 13:1–7

MY "LOVE" REPORT CARD

After reading St. Paul's "Hymn of Love" (above) give yourself a "grade" from A to F as a teacher would in school (but acting as your own self-critic) on each of the following areas. Share each of your responses with your group.

Patience   _____

Kindness   _____

Jealousy   _____

Conceit/Boasting   _____

Rudeness   _____

Selfishness   _____

Resentfulness   _____

Willingness to excuse, forgive others   _____

Doctrinal Connector: The Christian community finds its fullest expression when God's people assemble to celebrate a Eucharistic liturgy. Also what are traditionally called the four "marks" of the Church exemplify the Catholic community—that it is (1) "one" or has unity, (2) "holy," (3) "Catholic," embracing everyone, and (4) apostolic, tracing itself back to St. Peter and the early Christian community.

THE "THIRD" VATICAN COUNCIL

A council is a meeting of the pope, cardinals and bishops and leaders of the church to make important decisions for the entire church. The purpose of this exercise is to give you a feeling for both the universality (world-wide nature) and vitality of the Catholic Church.

Procedure: Your leader will assign you roles. After your role/group assignment, meet with your group for five minutes to discuss the agenda you wish to present to the council based on your own concerns and the needs of the group you represent. You are all delegates of the council. The pope and his cardinals should sit in front. They, too, have an agenda which they will present last—agendas should be presented in the order listed here. After the presentation of an agenda a group may ask the pope for no more than one ruling. When a request is made for a new ruling on church policy the pope must:

1. Allow a maximum of five minutes for discussion by the entire council.

2. Take a vote of the entire council: he must *consider* the vote but he isn't necessarily obliged to follow it.

3. Ask the advice of his cardinal-bishops.

4. Announce his decision publicly.

(Presentation of agendas should last no more than five minutes)

ROLES/GROUPS—number also indicates order of agenda:

1. One bishop from Bangladesh, which is one of the poorest third-world nations, one Arab, one priest from Ethiopia.

2. One bishop and two priests from the Soviet Union. (second world)

3. Three laywomen from Australia, the United States, and the United Kingdom. (first world)

4. A pope and two cardinals (bishops who assist the pope).

MINISTRY MIRROR

We have many parts in the one body, and all these parts have different functions. In the same way, though we are many, we are one body in union with Christ, and we are all joined to each other as different parts of one body. So we are to use our different gifts in accordance with the grace that God has given us. If our gift is to speak God's message, we should do it according to the faith that we have; if it is to serve, we should serve; if it is to teach, we should teach; if it is to encourage others, we should do so. Whoever shares with others should do it generously; whoever has authority should work hard; whoever shows kindness to others should do it cheerfully.

Romans 12:4–8

I. How do you see yourself? (fill in the space)

A talent you possess:	
A strength in your personality:	
A quality others admire in you:	
A form of service you feel you are (or would be) good at:	

II. Instead of sharing your responses about yourself the group should focus on one member at a time and tell that person how each of you see him or her in light of the four questions above. Every group member should talk to/about every other group member. See if what others say about you matches what you wrote about yourself. Most importantly, let what others say to you "sink in"; try to trust and believe your group.

Doctrinal Connector: Martin Luther, who led the Protestant Reformation, said that faith alone is necessary for salvation. Although Lutherans and Catholics today agree, the Church refuted Luther by saying that "good works" or Christian love and service are also necessary to be saved. "Apostolate" is the word that was used a generation ago for "ministry" (see James 2:14–26).

SOCIAL JUSTICE AWARENESS SURVEY

(Answer true or false to each question, i.e., if the statement is *generally* true or false for you.)

I am aware

1. because I watch the nightly news on TV _____
2. because I read world events in the daily newspaper _____
3. because I read one news magazine each week _____
4. of the workings of the welfare system in this country _____
5. of the connection between defense and the national budget (what percentage is spent) _____
6. of what "third world" means _____
7. of the Church's encyclicals on social justice _____
8. of meat consumption in the USA vis-à-vis other nations _____
9. of who my congressmen/women are _____
10. of what women's liberation is all about _____
11. of the difficulties experienced by at least one minority group in my locale _____
12. of the victimization of youth by the media and advertising world _____
13. of injustice in some group or community of which I am a member _____
14. of the issues in the next local or state election _____
15. of the connection of the right-to-life (anti-abortion movement) to the Gospel _____
16. of the basic contents of "The Challenge of Peace" document _____
17. of the arguments against capital punishment _____
18. of which political party I favor _____
19. of the meaning of "civil disobedience" _____
20. of what the Gospel wants me to do about justice and peace _____

(If you have answered "False" to four or more of these, your awareness level is in need of improvement.)

Doctrinal Connector: The virtue of justice is the constant and permanent determination to give everyone his or her due. It is a fundamental Christian and human virtue and lies at the very core of civilization.

PEACE QUESTIONNAIRE

Try to answer these briefly and truthfully; share answers with your group.

1. Are you a peaceful person within yourself? If so, what causes that? If not, what causes a lack of peace?

2. What techniques do you use when you want to become a more peaceful person?

3. Is there any line from the Bible or a religious song that makes you more peaceful? If so, what?

4. Do you see yourself as a source of peace or of disturbance within your home?

5. Do you see yourself as a peacemaker in any situations?

6. When you have differences or disagreements with others, how do you resolve them?

7. Do you enjoy violence in the movies and on TV?

8. Have you ever read the lives of any famous nonviolent leaders like Martin Luther King or Dorothy Day? Did you see the film "Gandhi"? How did it affect you?

9. As a Christian, what do you think your viewpoint should be about nuclear arms?

10. Do you feel you have any responsibility to act on your viewpoints?

11. Do you know what the bishops of the United States said in their letter *The Challenge of Peace?*

12. Do you see a connection between the Catholic Church's opposition to a nuclear arms race and its anti-abortion or "Right to Life" stand and stand against capital punishment (by the American bishops)?

MY MORALITY

Answer the following questions as truthfully and reflectively as you can and then share your responses with your group.

1. Is there or has there been an issue in which you have been involved where you have had to choose between right or wrong? (Pick something you're willing to share with this group.)
   What is it?

2. What steps did you follow in your process of making this moral decision?
   (1)

   (2)

   (3)

   (4)

3. Do you ever examine your behavior by pondering within yourself or discussing it with someone?

4. Does your religion have much to do with your moral choices? If so, in what way?

5. Do you think that young people ever use each other sexually?

6. Is there some moral question of our day which confuses you?

7. Do you see drug abuse as immoral? Why?

Doctrinal Connector: Morality is a term applied to human conduct. It is a norm which determines whether human actions are right and fitting or bad and unbefitting a follower of Jesus Christ. Moral acts must be considered within the context of their circumstances and their ends. The Pope and bishops provide guidance for the Church in matters of morals.

FRIENDS: MY "MORAL MIRROR"

We often judge a friend by his/her values, sense of morality. This reflects back to us what we ourselves value and cherish. To better understand your own sense of morality list three qualities you look for in a friendship, then share them with your group.

1.

2.

3.

What are your top three values in life?
Share with your group also.

1.

2.

3.

Sometimes our personal values separate us from friends. Briefly write down two situations in which you felt your own values conflicted with those of a friend(s). How did you handle these situations? Share one of them with your group.

PARENTS AND FAMILY LIFE

Complete the following and share your responses with your group:

1. What trait (strength or weakness) do you feel you inherit or have learned from

   your mother: _____

   your father: _____

2. Complete this statement: "I wish my parents would understand me when I . . ."

3. The thing that I think would bring more harmony, more happiness into my family would be:

In the space below write a paragraph to your parents (or parent) telling them the most important message you would like them to hear from you. (You are not required to share this with them but if you have the courage to do so the communication could be helpful.)

Doctrinal Connector: The centrality of family life within Christianity is summed up in Vatican II's Decree on the Laity: "The family has received from God its mission to be the first and vital cell of society. . . . For their part, young people would be wise to cultivate toward adults respect and trust. Although the young are naturally attracted to new things, they should exercise an intelligent regard for worthwhile traditions."

FAMILYGRAM

Diagram your immediate family, putting members close/far from you as symbols of how close/far you feel toward them. Explain your family-gram to your group:

Sample:

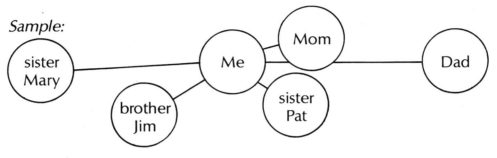

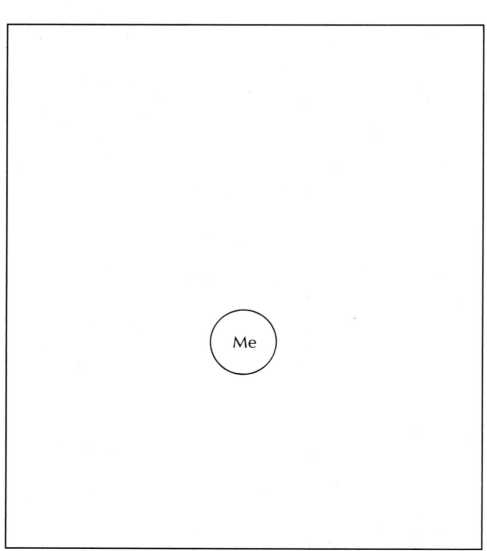

Rite of Enrollment

Procession

Candidates and sponsors should be a part of the entrance procession and sit in a prominent place together in the church.

After the liturgy of the word (concludes with the homily):

Leader (or D.R.E.):
Stands before the pastor.

Father, I present to you these baptized young Christians who seek to deepen their Christian commitment and become full members of their Church by receiving the sacrament of Confirmation. They have been faithfully attending preparation sessions over the past six months, have engaged in a service project to the community (and participated in a weekend retreat). As they enter into the final phase of their preparation I (we) ask that our parish community affirm and welcome them.

(Sponsors stand)

Pastor:
Dear sponsors of these young people: Are you willing to undertake the task of guiding these candidates in the final phase of their preparation for Confirmation?

Sponsors:
We are.

Pastor:
Do you promise to support them by your prayers and example not only during these next weeks but throughout their lifetime?

Sponsors:
We do.

Pastor:
(To group leader[s] or D.R.E.) And are you as their catechist(s) willing to verify for your parish community that there is a real sense of commitment to following Jesus' way of life within the Roman Catholic Church?

Leader(s) or D.R.E. *(standing):*
I am (we are).

(Candidates stand)

Pastor:
Young people of our parish: Are you willing to continue the process of Christian initiation begun in you at Baptism and continued in the Eucharist?

Candidates:
We are.

Pastor:
Do you understand that the sacrament of Confirmation symbolizes not a completion of your religious education but rather a mature commitment to continue to grow spiritually as Christian adults?

Candidates:
We do.

Pastor:
Then may God bring to completion in you the good work that has begun in Jesus Christ. I invite you to come forward and to enroll your name in our parish book of candidates. *(He then calls the name of each youth individually, who in turn enters the sanctuary with his or her sponsor and enrolls their names in the book on a table next to the altar. The page is headed: "I promise to faithfully complete the Confirmation process I have begun in order to follow Jesus Christ more closely as my Lord.")*

(When the last candidate has been enrolled the pastor invites the congregation to applaud.)

Prayers for the Candidates

(Included in the Prayer of the Faithful)

Pastor:
Let us pray for these young people as they enter the final phase of their preparation for Confirmation.

Lector:
For these young people that they feel in a concrete way the support of our parish community, let us pray to the Lord.

Congregation:
Lord, hear our prayer.

Lector:

That these young people have the awareness that they have been especially chosen by God to receive the grace of this sacrament, let us pray to the Lord.

Congregation:

Lord, hear our prayer.

Lector:

For the parents, sponsors, catechists and all who have contributed and will continue to contribute to the spiritual formation of these candidates, let us pray to the Lord.

Congregation:

Lord, hear our prayer.

Lector:

For each of us, that we will renew again today the commitment made at our own Confirmation, let us pray to the Lord.

Congregation:

Lord, hear our prayer.

Pastor:

Lord Jesus, we thank you for the witness here today of these beautiful young people who choose to follow you more closely. Give them your Spirit to guide, nourish and sustain them all the days of their lives.

(The Mass then continues with the Creed.)

"JOURNEY IN THE SPIRIT"
SPONSOR/CANDIDATE MINI-RETREAT

A time in my life that I felt God's intervention (or if you think you haven't had that experience you may write about a time when you felt you needed God but God remained at a distance).

Spirit of God,
Enlighten me.
Grace of God,
move me.
Heart of God,
electrify me.
Compassion of God,
touch me.
Hand of God,
heal me.
Passion of God,
stir me.
Mind of God,
Counsel me.

From
*Prayers for a
New Generation*

**EXERCISE #1
LIFE GRAPH**

LIFE GRAPH

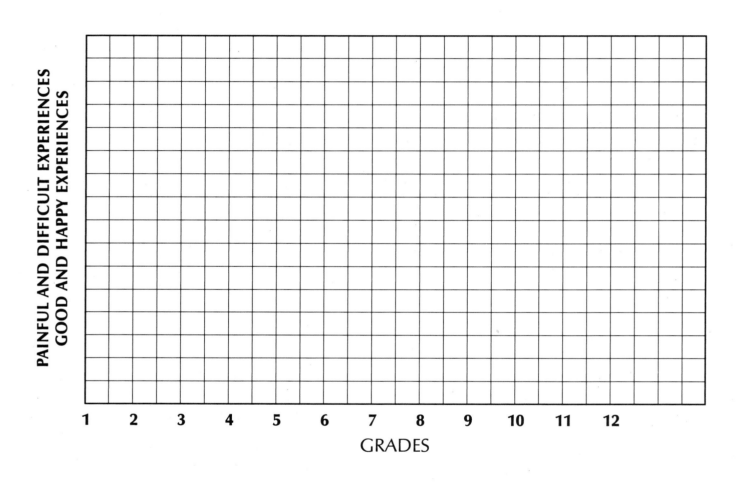

EXERCISE #2
MASKS

1. A "mask" I wear in school (or in public) is:

2. A "mask" I wear in my family is:

3. A "mask" I wear with my friends is:

EXERCISE #3
"JESUS"

Write your answers thoughtfully to these questions and then share them with your group.

1. How did you arrive at your own "image" or picture of Jesus?

2. Do you feel you have had an "experience" of Jesus Christ in your life? Where? When?

3. Do you feel you have a personal relationship with Jesus?

4. Do you want to get closer to Jesus? If you do, will it change you?

ARE YOU STILL UNSURE ABOUT YOUR CHOICE?

Now that you have completed so much of the CHOICE process and have had the experience of Christian community on your retreat, are you ready to choose to be an adult follower of Jesus Christ? Are you ready to receive the sacrament of Confirmation? If you *still* have any doubts or confusion the first task is to analyze their nature. Are they actually doubts about your faith or are they just the "last minute jitters" about an important step in your life? To be a little nervous about serious decisions is very human and very normal. If they are in fact doubts about your faith are they more about the existence of God or do they revolve more around an inner fear to make such a heavy commitment? If the latter, remember that the Church is a "hospital for sinners, not a rest home for saints." In other words, it isn't that you must always succeed in being a good Christian—it's that you must simply commit yourself to *try* to become one. Our compassionate God does not demand instant perfection on the day of Confirmation! Growing in goodness and holiness is the task of a lifetime.

If you have any confusion or doubts at this stage about receiving this sacrament you really need to talk them out: with your friends who are at the same stage in the CHOICE process; perhaps with your parents, or priest or youth minister; and definitely with your sponsor.

(In the event that you choose not to receive the sacrament at this time don't feel badly or guilty about it. Maybe you just aren't ready for the commitment or maybe the Holy Spirit needs to work more within you. Remember that we said this process isn't a "graduation." If you choose not to receive Confirmation at this time after the energy you have put into its preparation do not think of yourself as a "Confirmation drop-out." There is no such creature. God works within the soul of each person in his own time and we need to recognize and respect that uniqueness in each other. If you decide to delay reception of the sacrament you will need to discuss that eventually not only with your sponsor but also with your parents, your group leader and your parish priest. Whatever choice you make know that God is right around the next corner of your life.)

Penance Service

Sponsors and Confirmation candidates gather at the parish church.

Opening hymn suggestion: "Hosea" (Weston Priory)

First Reading
(Read by a candidate)
Psalm 73:21-26

> When my thoughts were bitter
>   and my feelings were hurt,
> I was as stupid as an animal;
>   I did not understand you.
> Yet I always stay close to you,
>   and you hold me by the hand.
> You guide me with your instruction
>   and at the end you will receive me with
>   honor.
> What else do I have in heaven but you?
>   Since I have you, what else could I want
>   on earth?
> My mind and my body may grow weak,
>   but God is my strength;
>   he is all I ever need.

Second Reading
(Read by a sponsor)
Luke 15:1-7

One day when many tax collectors and other outcasts came to listen to Jesus, the Pharisees and the teachers of the Law started grumbling, "This man welcomes outcasts and even eats with them!" So Jesus told them this parable:

"Suppose one of you has a hundred sheep and loses one of them—what does he do? He leaves the other ninety-nine sheep in the pasture and goes looking for the one that got lost until he finds it. When he finds it, he is so happy that he puts it on his shoulders and carries it back home. Then he calls his friends and neighbors together and says to them, 'I am so happy I found my lost sheep. Let us celebrate!' In the same way, I tell you, there will be more joy in heaven over one sinner who repents than over ninety-nine respectable people who do not need to repent."

Third Reading:
(Read by a deacon or priest)
Luke 15:11-32

The Lost Son
Jesus went on to say, "There was once a man who had two sons. The younger one said to him, 'Father, give me my share of the property now.' So the man divided his property between his two sons. After a few days the younger son sold his part of the property and left home with the money. He went to a country far away, where he wasted his money in reckless living. He spent everything he had. Then a severe famine spread over that country, and he was left without a thing. So he went to work for one of the citizens of that country, who sent him out to his farm to take care of the pigs. He wished he could fill himself with the bean pods the pigs ate, but no one gave him anything to eat. At last he came to his senses and said, 'All my father's hired workers have more than they can eat, and here I am about to starve! I will get up and go to my father and say, "Father, I have sinned against God and against you. I am no longer fit to be called your son; treat me as one of your hired workers."' So he got up and started back to his father.

"He was still a long way from home when his father saw him; his heart was filled with pity, and he ran, threw his arms around his son, and kissed him. 'Father,' the son said, 'I have sinned against God and against you. I am no longer fit to be called your son.' But the father called to his servants. 'Hurry!' he said. 'Bring the best robe and put it on him. Put a ring on his finger and shoes on his feet. Then go and get the prize calf and kill it, and let us celebrate with a feast! For this son of mine was dead, but now he is alive; he was lost, but now he has been found.'

And so the feasting began.

"In the meantime the older son was out in the field. On his way back, when he came close to the house, he heard the music and dancing. So he called one of the servants and asked him, 'What's going on?' 'Your brother has come back home,' the servant answered, 'and your father has killed the prize calf, because he got him back safe and sound.' The older brother was so angry that he would not go into the house; so his father came out and begged him to come in. But he spoke back to his father, 'Look, all these years I have worked for you like a slave, and I have never disobeyed your orders. What have you given me? Not even a goat for me to have a feast with my friends! But this son of yours wasted all your property on prostitutes, and when he comes back home you kill the prize calf for him!' 'My son,' the father answered, 'you are always here with me, and everything I have is yours. But we had to celebrate and be happy, because your brother was dead, but now he is alive; he was lost, but now he has been found.' "

Recorded Meditation Song (Church lights dimmed). *Suggestion:* "Sorry Is the Hardest Word" (Elton John)

Brief Homily
By a priest on the need for forgiveness and the significance of this service prior to Easter and the celebration of Confirmation.

Individual Confessions
Recorded hymns or classical music should be played softly while individuals receive the sacrament of Reconciliation. When all are finished the priest invites the congregation to stand.

Priest:
My brothers and sisters, let us rejoice that our God gives us a sacrament which wipes away sin, softens our hearts, and gives us the grace of a closer union with him and with each other. Let us pray for the needs of all in our community on this special night.

(Either a group of candidates can have prepared special intercessions—about six or seven—*or* the priest can invite spontaneous prayers from all assembled.)

Priest:
Dear Lord, you have heard our needs through these intercessions and those still bottled up in our hearts. Hear us, we beg you, and be gentle with us, for you are our Shepherd and we are your sheep. Amen.

Closing Hymn
Suggestion: "Here I Am, Lord" (St. Louis Jesuits)

Procedure of Receiving Sacrament (review)

1. Examine your conscience—in your mind and heart review your life since your last confession. Is there any serious sin? Are there patterns that have crept into your life which are not very Christian (e.g., always yelling at a younger brother or sister)?

2. Enter the reconciliation room. You may either sit before the priest or kneel behind him.

3. Tell the priest how long it has been since your last confession; then tell him your sins.

4. Recite an act of contrition or sorrow for your sin. (You may use: "O my God, I'm heartily sorry for having offended you who are worthy of all my love. I promise with the help of your grace to amend my life. Amen.")

5. Receive the absolution of the priest (he makes the sign of the cross saying your sins are forgiven).

6. After leaving say the prayers the priest has given you as a penance; if he has given you an action to perform you will have to wait for the appropriate time.

THE HOLY SPIRIT

The word "spirit" is *ruah* in Hebrew. To trace the use of this term throughout the Bible or "salvation history" pass a Bible around the group. Each member should find/read one passage and then pass the book on to the next person.

1. Genesis 1:1–2
2. Genesis 2:7
3. Isaiah 61:1
4. Luke 1:35
5. Matthew 3:13
6. Luke 4:18
7. John 14:16–17
8. Acts 1:8
9. Romans 8:9–11
10. 1 Corinthians 2:10–15
11. Ephesians 4:30–32
12. Galatians 5:22–26

"Fruits of the Spirit" (Galatians 5:22–23)

In this last Scripture passage we read the results (or "fruits") of a life lived in God's spirit: love, joy, peace, patience, kindness, goodness, faithfulness, humility and self-control. A person who possesses these characteristics gives evidence of being close to God.
    Respond to these questions in your group:

1. Do you know someone in whose life the "fruits of the Holy Spirit" are very much in evidence?

2. Are there times when these "fruits" are present in you?

3. What is an obstacle to the "fruits" being present more often in your life?

Doctrinal Connector: The Holy Spirit (sometimes called "Holy Ghost") is the third person of the Blessed Trinity. He is the "sanctifier" because he makes us holy by the graces and virtues he gives us. He is also called the "Comforter" because he continually comforts and nourishes the Church.

THE HOLY SPIRIT: CHALLENGE TO WITNESS

In this session we wish to get a "feel" for the Old Testament prophets who, strengthened with the Spirit of God, spoke out in society in behalf of God. At Confirmation you too will be receiving a strengthening grace to help you to be a witness to Jesus Christ. Pass the Bible around your group and take turns reading from these sections of the prophets' stories. (Jonah is fictional but was written to teach us some very important lessons.)

1. Amos 8:4–10
2. Jonah 1
3. Jonah 2
4. Jonah 3
5. Jonah 4
6. Hosea 2:2–13
7. Jeremiah 1:4–10
8. Jeremiah 18:5–12
9. Psalm 137 (The Israelites are taken captive in Babylon)
10. Ezekiel 37

Share your responses to these questions with your group:

1. Do you feel there are heroes and prophets of God in our own day? If so, whom would you name?

2. Did you ever feel moved by God's spirit to go "against the crowd" or speak out in behalf of justice? If so, share the experience with your group.

Doctrinal Connector: "God continues to manifest Himself through the Holy Spirit at work in the world, and especially in the Church. Christ, risen and living, is present to believers through the power of the Spirit. . . . The Spirit's actions also make believers sensitive to God's promptings in their hearts, moving them to respond and bear witness to Him so that others, too, may come to know the Lord." (National Catechetical Directory, #54)

GROWTH ESSAY

In the space below write a short essay about how you feel God's Spirit has grown in you these past six months through the weekly sessions, retreats, journal writing, liturgy and meetings with your sponsor.

Confirmation Rehearsal/"Waiting Prayer Service"

Lord, you have examined me and you know me.
You know everything I do;
    from far away you understand all my thoughts.
You see me, whether I am working or resting;
    you know all my actions.
Even before I speak,
    you already know what I will say.
You are all around me on every side; you protect me with your power.
Your knowledge of me is too deep; it is beyond my understanding.

Where could I go to escape from you?
Where could I get away from your presence?
If I went up to heaven, you would be there;
    if I lay down in the world of the dead, you would be there.
If I flew away beyond the east
    or lived in the farthest place in the west,
    you would be there to lead me,
    you would be there to help me.
I could ask the darkness to hide me
    or the light around me to turn into night,
    but even darkness is not dark for you,
    and the night is as bright as the day.
Darkness and light are the same to you.

You created every part of me;
    you put me together in my mother's womb.
I praise you because you are to be feared;
    all you do is strange and wonderful.
I know it with all my heart.
When my bones were being formed,
    carefully put together in my mother's womb,
    when I was growing there in secret,
    you knew that I was there—
    you saw me before I was born.
The days allotted to me had all been recorded in your book,
    before any of them ever began.
O God, how difficult I find your thoughts;
    how many of them there are!
If I counted them, they would be more than the grains of sand.
When I awake, I am still with you.

Examine me, O God, and know my mind;
    test me, and discover my thoughts.
Find out if there is any evil in me
    and guide me in the everlasting way.

From Psalm 139